Mighty Raptors

Adult Coloring Book

Natalie Totire

CourageLit
www.couragelit.com
e-mail: ntcreations@live.com

Printed by CreateSpace
www.createspace.com

All scripture quotations are taken from the Holy Bible, New International Version
THE HOLY BIBLE, NEW INTERNATIONAL VERSION®, NIV®
Copyright © 1973, 1978, 1984, 2011 by Biblica, Inc.® Used by permission. All rights reserved worldwide.

Here is the book "God's Mighty Raptors" in a nutshell with pictures that you can color. As you color, you can learn interesting facts summarized about each one of them.

The introductory pages are based on ancient Native American or Egyptian paintings. All other images were based on Natalie Totire's paintings and photos.

Introduction

Birds are wonderful creatures. Our Bibles tell us in Genesis 1-2 that God created them on the 5th day of creation. When God created the world, He said it was very good. The fossil record shows us a much wider variety of birds, reptiles, insects, and mammals than we see today. Powerful dinosaurs stomped on the ground, and dazzling birds in a wide array of colors flew and glided in the air or ran across the ground. We learn from nature that God loves variety. After the fall of man, death and disease entered the world, and some animals became meat-eaters. Birds of prey still have wonderful attributes we can learn from. Enjoy learning about God's fingerprints in each one of them as you color in the details of their wonderful feathers.

Extinct birds of prey include the unusual Archeopteryx and the 25 foot long
Argentavis Magnificens, which was the largest flying bird ever known to mankind.

One of the largest known eagles, now extinct, was the Haast's Eagle of New Zealand. It was twice the size of the largest living eagle today. It hunted the Moa, a large, flightless bird, now also extinct.

Eagles can soar for miles, and when courting, love to perform all sorts of flying acrobats.
The Bible tells us in Isaiah 40:31, "They that wait upon the Lord shall renew their strength.
They shall mount up with wings and fly like eagles." NIV.

Eagles build large nests, with Bald eagles ranking the largest. The largest Bald Eagle nest ever recorded was in Florida, and it reached 20 high and 10 feet across!

Most eagles take up to four or five years to become completely mature. Although they can fly within a few months, their adult plumage does not come until years later. It also takes them a lot of practice to become skilled hunters, and many eagles do not survive their first year.

Golden Eagles are the most widespread of all eagles. They range throughout Europe, Asia, and western North America and mostly prey on small mammals. When attracting a mate, they can make sky-dances and astonishing sky dives at 200 mph.

The Bald Eagle is a fish eagle, and fish are its primary diet. It is found throughout the United States and Canada and has become the national bird of the United States. The African Fish Eagle is very similar to the Bald Eagle in both appearance and diet.

The Bateleur is one of God's most unusual and colorful eagles, and it is so-called because of its amazing graceful way of flying. The word "bateleur" means "juggler" in French.

The African Crowned Eagle, also called the African Crowned Hawk-Eagle, is a powerful and beautifully colored eagle. The crest on its head is what gives it its name.

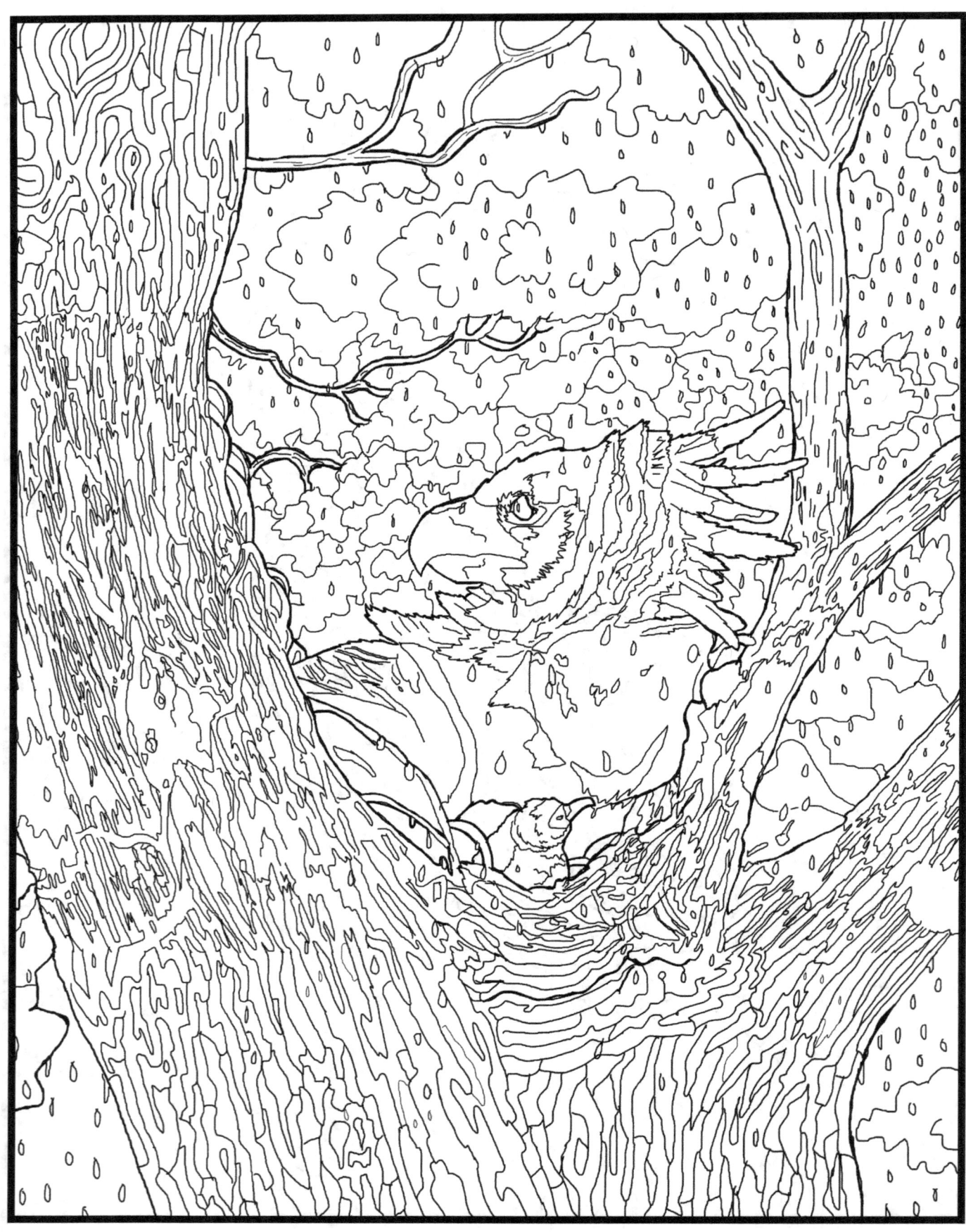

The huge Harpy Eagle of South America is a monster of the jungle, preying on monkeys and sloths. However, Harpy Eagles are good parents. The mother protects her chick during a fierce tropical storm.

This rare, mysterious eagle lives deep in the woods of the Philippines. It is called the Philippine Eagle. It is the national bird of the country and one of the largest eagles in the world. Statistics report that there are less than 500 left in the wild.

Owls are extremely silent flyers. Their feathers were designed to withstand sound. A mouse cannot hear an owl flying overhead.

One of the smallesst owls in the world is the Elf Owl, which stands only six inches tall. It lives in the desert badlands of the United States, eats insects, and will often take refuge inside cactuses.

Barred Owls have been increasing in number across the United States, sometimes breeding with the Spotted Owls. They are best distinguished by their call: "Who cooks for you. Who cooks for you all."

Short-eared Owls live in the United States, Canada, Europe, and Asia. Unlike most other owls, they prefer to roost in tundras, prairies, pastures, and grasslands. Another unusual feature is that they may hunt and cooperate in groups as many as 30 or more.

Spotted Owls are found in the western part of the United States. They live and nest in large, old evergreen trees, such as redwoods and hemlocks. They have been threatened due to deforestation, but are now protected by law.

The Great Gray Owl's feathers act like a satellite disk. It has hearing so well, that it can hear a mouse at a distance scuttling about under the snow.   Great Grays are the largest owls in the Northeastern United States.

Screech Owls are small, up to 8 inch tall. They live in the Eastern United States, but are very similar to and are believed to be closely related to the European Scops Owls. Screech Owls come in a wide variety of races, such as red, brown, or gray,

The Great Horned Owl is king of the forest, standing 18 inches tall. It lives in both North and South America. It preys on all sorts of small birds and mammals, including the striped skunk. Skunk spray does not drive away the owl because it has no sense of smell.

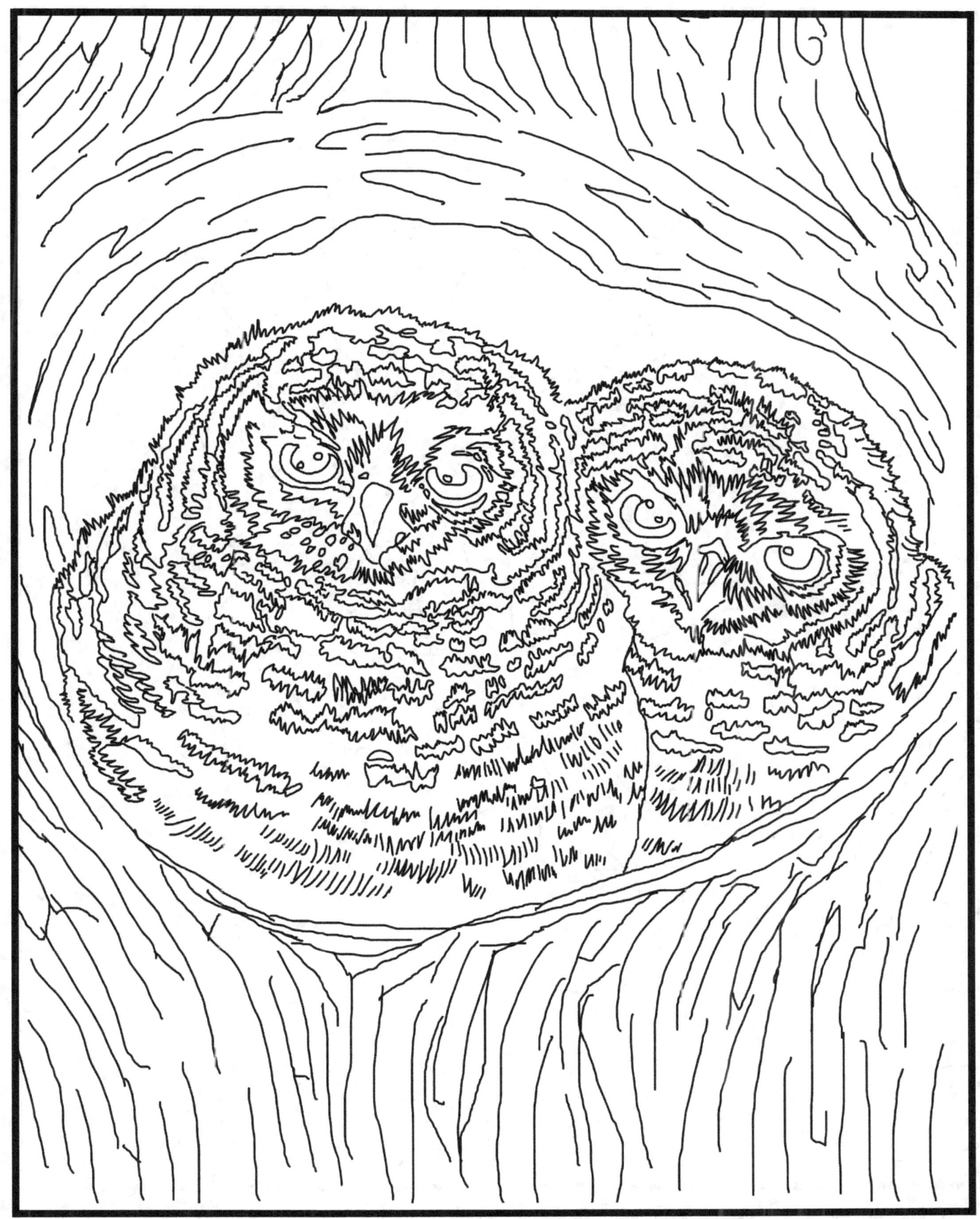

Young Great Horned Owls have a fluffy appearance. They grow fast and are able to climb about the tree before they are able to fly.

Burrowing Owls are one of the few birds that live subterranean and nest underground. They usually take over old prairie dog holes.

The Saw-whet Owl is one of the smallest owls of eastern North America. They are strictly camouflaged and are hard to find, but one may find the owl from surrounding songbirds making a commotion. These owls are surprisingly tame, if found.

Barn Owls are found in almost every continent except Antarctica. They are good rodent-catchers and are notorious for storing up prey around the nest for a rainy day. The largest cache ever found on record was 189 voles!

The Eurasian Eagle Owl is one of the largest owls in the world, which stands 23-29 inches tall. It is a powerful owl which can prey on Snowy Owls, Tawny Owls, Goshawks, and other birds as large as herons.

Hawks and Falcons

The Osprey is also known as the fish hawk. Its oily feathers are water-proof, making it easy to dive in and out of water. In some places, mankind has built posts on top of telephone poles to encourage Osprey nesting.

The Red-tailed Hawk is one of the most common and widespread of hawks within North America. It is called a Buteo Hawk because of its long wings and broad tail, making it able to soar like an eagle. It is highly adaptable in cities and suburbs.

The Red-shouldered Hawk is a favorite for bird watchers. It lives deep in the woods near swamps and is supurbly colored. To attract a mate, the male will perform acrobatic sky dances.

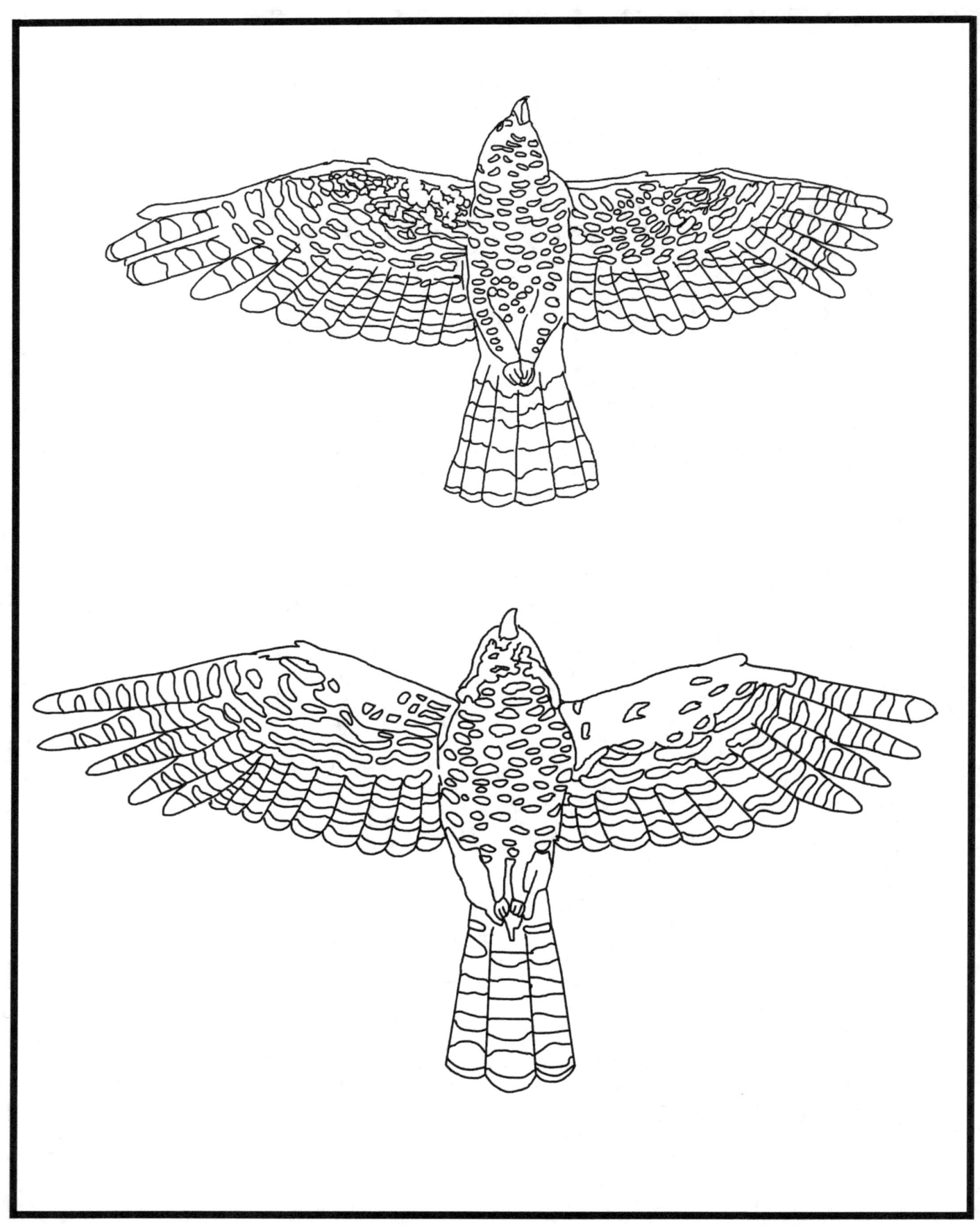

Accipactor Hawks, such as the Cooper's and the Sharp-shinned Hawks, have smaller wings, better for maneuvering than soaring. Sometimes bird-watchers have difficulty telling these two apart. The Sharp-shinned Hawk (top) is smaller, with a square tail. The Cooper's Hawk (bottom) has a more rounded tail.

The Cooper's Hawk has been known as the "Chicken Hawk", and farmers disliked them. Further studies showed that these hawks preyed more on mice and rats that ate the grain than on livestock. Juvenile hawks have brown streaks, and mature hawks are gray with brick-red eyes.

The Goshawk is the largest and most powerful accipactor hawk, measuring two-feet long. Its name means "Goosehawk" because it is able to take down geese, but it can also take down grouses, medium sized hawks, and owls.

Unlike most other hawks, the Broadwing Hawk will migrate in flocks, usually found in the United States near the ocean or the Great Lakes. These flocks may circle together in thermals that some people call "kettles" or "boils" because it resembles boiling water.

The Peregrine Falcon is found widespread throughout the world. It is the fastest animal today on planet earth, reaching up to speeds of 82 mph when swooping down on prey, but it was also recorded of reaching 230 mph when trying to catch a lure.

The Prairie Falcon only lives in the United States. It is highly nomadic. Although similar, it is not as trainable as the Peregrine Falcon. Falconers who keep falcons for hunting have been able to crossbreed the two.

The American Kestrel is one of the most colorful falcons. The male (top) differs from the female (bottom, on perch) in that it has blue-gray wings and lacks the striped tail. Kestrels have good eyesight and can see ultraviolet light . They can also hover over their prey.

The White-tailed Kite resembles a falcon both in shape and size. It is white while its wings are black and white. Like the Kestrel, the kite is also able to hover before it grasps its prey.

Vultures

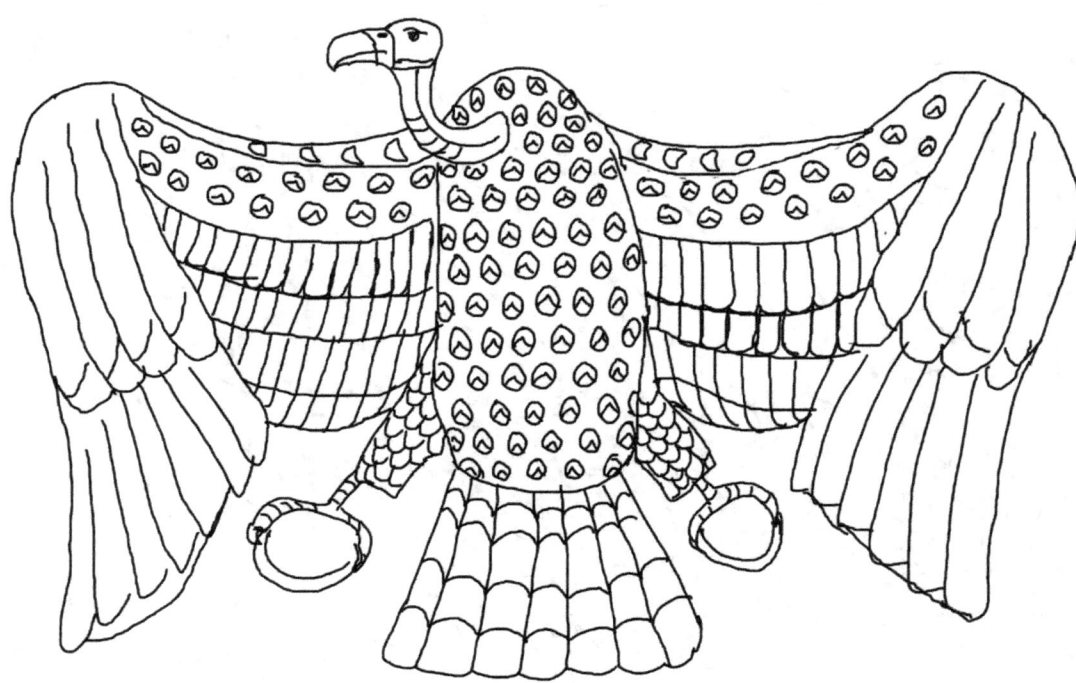

Vulture may seem repulsive, but they are God's cleanup crew, ridding the environment from diseases that might have emerged from decaying carcasses. The Turkey Vulture is quite common in the United States. It finds dead animals through its very keen sense of smell. Up close, its black wings have a green and purple sheen.

All other vultures move out of the way when the powerful King Vulture comes. It is usually the first to eat its share of meat. King Vultures are very bright and colorful, with purples, bright red, orange, and yellow coloring on its face and neck.

The California Condor is one of the rarest condors in the world, and it is among the largest of the flying birds in the United States. Human intervention is slowly helping it make a comeback. The similar Andean Condor of South America is the largest flying bird in the world, measuring up to four feet long with a wingspan of 10-12 feet.

Vultures that live in Europe, Asia and Africa are called "Old World Vultures", and they differ from the American "New World" Vultures. The Egyptian Vulture is an Old World Vulture. It is smaller and weaker than its counterparts, but it is very intelligent. It knows how to use rocks as tools to open ostrich eggs.

The Eurasian Griffon Vulture is found widespread throughout Europe and Northern Israel. It works together and cooperate in its search for food. The similar Ruppel's Griffon Vulture of Central Africa is the highest flying bird recorded, with an altitude of 36,000 feet.

The Lammergeier finishes what other vultures have left of the carcass. About 90% of its diet consists of bones, which it picks up and breaks. It's stomach content is so acidic, it digests both bones and tortoise shells. Many have a pinkish hue on their necks from rubbing against the rocks.

About the Author

Natalie Totire always had fascination in learning about animals and grew up watching Nature programs. She graduated with a degree in Educational Ministries from Moody Bible Institute, where she researched on the book of Genesis, but became increasingly interested in writing and illustrating for children.

Natalie later took a correspondence course from the Institute of Children's Literature followed by working as a Newspaper Journalist while attending Triton College. She is now a Phi Theta Kappa member, and her paintings won numerous awards at the DuPage Art League. Natalie works directly with children at day cares, before and after school care, Sunday School, and mission trips.

For many years, Natalie wrote fiction books, but later she shifted her interest into writing nonfiction. She had a continued interest in animals which eventually led to the making of this book.

This book is based on the larger book "God's Mighty Raptors" which gives even further information about individual birds of prey.